25 SALESBOOSTERS

25 SALESBOOSTERS

An arsenal of powerful techniques for elevating your income

Thane Crossley

Copyright © 2015 Thane Crossley
All rights reserved.

ISBN: 150885713X
ISBN 13: 9781508857136
Library of Congress Control Number: 2015904178
CreateSpace Independent Publishing Platform, North Charleston, South Carolina

Table of Contents

	Introduction	vii
Chapter 1	Gratitude Sells	1
Chapter 2	The Prosperity Question	5
Chapter 3	Turn Mind Power into Sales Power	9
Chapter 4	Money Galore	13
Chapter 5	Elevate Your Sales Dialogue	17
Chapter 6	Stay Upbeat	21
Chapter 7	Close More Sales	25
Chapter 8	Say No to Rejection	31
Chapter 9	Be Positively Negative	35
Chapter 10	Restore Your Confidence	39
Chapter 11	Sharpen Your Focus	43
Chapter 12	Walk This Way	47
Chapter 13	Find Career Joy	51
Chapter 14	Raise Your Energy	55
Chapter 15	Mend Relationships	59
Chapter 16	Eight Ways to "New"	63
Chapter 17	Copy Right	67
Chapter 18	The Five Whys	71
Chapter 19	First Calls	75
Chapter 20	Take Action	79

Chapter 21	Seller Beware	83
Chapter 22	Check Your Altitude	87
Chapter 23	Small Gains	91
Chapter 24	Relationships Plus	95
Chapter 25	Feel Wealthy	99

Introduction

Are you getting the most from your sales efforts? What else can you do to excel? This book explains simple yet powerful actions you can take to move beyond the competition. As you strengthen your skills, you will build an exciting, vibrant future.

The information contained in these pages is based on coaching consultations with thousands of sales professionals. From these conversations, twenty-five common themes emerged. If we were meeting in person at my Toronto office, you would receive the same advice and guidance that is provided here. Chapters are deliberately presented in an order and sequence that is optimal for your development.

As a psychologist, I am in constant awe of the power, creativity, and resiliency of our minds. To assist you in best integrating the clearly explained concepts, the book is written in hypnotic language. When entranced, a person absorbs what is being stated on a deeper level.

Capitalize on your time investment by reading each page slowly and thoughtfully. Carefully consider what is being said. Apply the learnings for your ever-increasing benefit.

I recommend rereading one chapter on a biweekly basis. With gradual and consistent practice, the helpful principles will become your truth. Devote ten minutes each professional day and in a year you will be amazed how far you have come.

Sales is an incredible profession that offers rewards on multiple levels. Hidden in plain view on the pages that follow are some of the world's most effective secrets for sales mastery, as well as for great success in life. I am indebted to our clients for helping refine and perfect the presented techniques. Discover for yourself how you can use them to your advantage.

Thane Crossley
Toronto
April 2015

1

Gratitude Sells

It has been a privilege interviewing and coaching hundreds of account managers. Many of these accomplished professionals have commented on how grateful they are for their success. They deeply appreciate the business that customers have given them and the associated financial rewards.

The gratitude appreciative salespeople experience provides a subtle yet powerful edge over their competitors. Selling is easier and more enjoyable when goodwill is radiated to others.

How are you feeling today? Is gratitude your underlying emotion? Are you grateful for what you have achieved? Look around; do you recognize what is available to you?

We tend to take what we have, and what we see in the world, for granted. Our brains and our thinking are oriented more with what's coming next rather than how we can best appreciate what we have now.

What could you be grateful for? When five sales executives were queried, they reflected for a moment before saying:

- *"I am grateful for my wonderful daughter."*
- *"For the opportunity to sell a great product."*

- *"For the awakening of a new day."*
- *"For my family and friends."*
- *"I am grateful for the success I have achieved."*

Having a genuine feeling of gratitude is most important. It can't be faked or forced. You either feel it or you don't. Feeling a little gratitude about something is a great place to start. Knowing the answer to "What are you most grateful for now?" is a solid beginning.

Of course, gratitude is easy to experience when things are going well. When your sales, and your commissions, are on top of the world, who wouldn't be happy, who wouldn't be grateful? But when customers and sales are sparse, who in their right mind would think of feeling gratitude? Why should you be grateful for a lack of business?

Top salespeople have told us that gratitude felt in the moment, for life's gifts, helped them to be in the right state of mind to enthusiastically pursue new opportunities. This was especially so when the chips were down.

You may have noticed in your own life that it is usually difficult to quickly move from a mind-set of being discouraged to a state of feeling all charged up and ready to go. It is easier to gladly flow from one river of abundance to another. Expressed another way, gratitude in the mind leads to gratitude in the field. When you are grateful now, new sales opportunities to pursue become apparent.

Over your career to date, you have no doubt tried out new approaches and techniques, incorporating those that have worked for you into your current recipe for success. Do the same with the powerful concept of gratitude. Try it out for a week. See if it contributes to you feeling more alive, more energetic, more in touch with your true capabilities and potential.

A few times during the day, remind yourself of the things you appreciate about your sales world. Finish this sentence: "I greatly appreciate…(my top customers)." When you say this, feel gratitude. First think it in your mind, then feel it in your heart. Focus on this feeling for a moment and imagine it spreading out from your center, infusing every cell of your being. Let this infusion of gratitude enhance your sales spirit.

You may be surprised to rediscover that simple and sincere gratitude will get your game up to speed quickly and effectively. Continuous gratitude in your mind, as a backdrop to your day-to-day sales activities, will help you and others to experience the best of yourself. Your efforts will resonate with a higher quality.

Simple and sincere gratitude is a golden key to greater prosperity, hidden in plain sight for those whose career journey is ever upward. Will you come along?

2

The Prosperity Question

"It's unattainable," said Susan. *"Are we not just setting ourselves up to get knocked down?"*

In response, Stan, the team leader, replied, *"I understand—but let's think about how it could be done."*

Len piped in, *"Stan, you know there is no way we can do this. Let's be realistic about what we can accomplish. Our market is shrinking by three percent each year. The company has set our target fifteen percent above our last quarter. It's simply impossible to achieve. What if we fail?"*

As the other account managers expressed their doubts and reservations, Stan persisted. *"I hear your concerns. But let's switch off our rational minds for a few minutes and just imagine we have met head office's targets. What if we are successful? Be there now. Imagine that space. How would we feel? What would we say to one another? How would our faces look?"*

Slowly, Stan began to shift the group's focus from rational doubt to fanciful imagination.

Gus said, *"OK, if we did it, it would feel empowering. We would be proud."*

"We would be wearing big smiles," added Jan.

Even Susan remarked, *"What if we really met these targets? It would feel amazing."*

Stan noticed a different energy level in the room. In their imaginations his team shifted from facing an impossible scenario to an achievable one.

The more the team entertained this "what if we did it?" mind-set, the more enthusiastic and engaged they became. They started to brainstorm about actions they had taken in their mind's eye to achieve the formerly impossible targets. Many of their ideas were practical and imminently doable:

- *"We recommitted to our existing customers."*
- *"We gave new customers two compelling reasons to try our product."*
- *"We earned our competitors' share of the market."*

This narrative is a factual representation of what happened in a Southwestern Ontario town. The team's target was 15 percent–plus in a shrinking market. The group increased sales by 18 percent over three quarters and continued to demonstrate this elevated level of performance. The team leader understood the power and utility of asking the right questions. Questions that led to abundance. Questions that left a scarcity mind-set behind.

In challenging, difficult situations, what type of questions are circling in your head? Although it is natural and normal to ask one's self, "What if I fail?", is this type of question helpful? Does it open up new avenues?

Psychologists tell us that the mind essentially works through the association of ideas. That is, one thought leads to another of equal or greater valence. If the first troubling thought is a negative one, the probability of the next thought continuing in the same direction is increased. Soon, we may have planted an entire garden of weeds. Or perhaps we have merely raised the perceived height of the original barrier we were facing. While we all think in this way from time to time, it is important to recognize that limiting questions produce limiting results. Our sales futures can be determined by the questions we ask ourselves today.

Of course, a few negative questions every once in a while along with a practical backup plan are always good insurance against worst case scenarios. However, too much emphasis and sustained attention on the downside of things may very well prevent a person from looking beyond the problem or obstacle. You do not want to preempt your success. Keep your attention focused upward, on the goals you truly aspire to achieve.

Let's recognize limiting questions for what they are and express them a different way. Here are examples of limiting or scarcity questions along with their expansive (prosperity) counterparts:

<u>**Scarcity Questions**</u>

1. What if I don't make the sale?

2. What if the client is difficult to persuade?

<u>**Prosperity Questions**</u>

1. What if the customer says yes?

2. What if I enthusiastically handle all objections?

3. What if the buyer wants only the best price?

3. What if I sell on added value?

4. What if the competition is too tough?

4. What if I focus on all the things I do well?

5. What if I fail?

5. What if I excel?

Endeavour to be more aware of the questions you are asking yourself. When you catch yourself asking a scarcity question, recognize it as such. Then ask the question in a way that is more aligned with prosperity. A way that enables prosperous thinking.

As you gently and enthusiastically practice this easy technique, it will become your habit, your truth. The accompanying sales revitalization will set you free to reach the success you desire.

3

Turn Mind Power into Sales Power

Regardless of your sales experience or the product you are selling, you will be able to increase your success by following the suggestions in this chapter. The tips provided here are simple and powerful. In fact, the information may seem too good to be true. And yet, as you apply what you have learned, what you are about to read will become your truth. You will be convinced by the results you obtain.

The source of your soon-to-be-experienced prosperity resides in your mind; your deeper or subconscious mind, to be exact, which complements your surface or conscious mind. For conceptual purposes, it is convenient to describe these two marvelous entities as if they were separate. They are really just different levels of awareness within your multifaceted, multitalented "one" master mind.

Your surface mind is where you do most of your thinking and analyzing. It is the mind that, during your waking hours, is systematically processing information. Meanwhile your deeper mind, among other things, takes care of your physiology, making sure your organs and systems are functioning properly. Pause for a moment and consider the level of sophistication and intelligence required to keep your body operating. If you had to think about how to maintain your heartbeat or how to regulate your metabolism, you would not have much time for anything else. Nor would it be much fun.

All the great philosophies and religions of the world agree that the deeper mind is very powerful. It possesses superhuman qualities and capabilities that far transcend our understanding. The omniscience of this mind has been acknowledged by scientists, neurologists, and psychologists. You were born with this mind so that you may experience life more fully.

Your deeper mind is resident to a creative faculty that defies reason and goes far beyond common sense. Have you had the experience of setting your alarm clock and waking up a few minutes before it went off? How was it possible for your deeper mind to keep track of the time?

Utilizing the right techniques, you can evoke the support of your deeper mind to help you achieve your sales objectives. To be successful in this endeavor you need to be clear on what you want to achieve, be precise and diligent in practicing and applying the principles we are going to present, and to continue with your normal sales efforts.

Be clear on what you want to achieve. After thinking about your goals and targets, write down one sales objective that you would be happy to accomplish. For example, "I have increased my sales by seven percent over a four-month period," or "I have brought in the World Source account I have been working on."

Note how these sample statements or affirmations are expressed. For the best results, they should be worded as if these have already occurred. As if you have accomplished that which you desire.

Over the next few days, give careful thought and consideration to what you would like to accomplish. Jot down a worthwhile goal that you feel excited about. Express your objective as if it were already a reality. You may want to revise the statement several times so that it clearly reflects what you truly want.

While technology is wonderful, recording your message in your own writing or printing style is preferable to an electronic entry. Optionally, it is also a great idea to add a drawing or sketch to the words, showing the desired result as you visualize it. The quality of the drawing is unimportant. The desire and feeling in your heart are paramount.

As you are drifting into sleep at night, slowly say the desired goal to yourself exactly as you have written it. Repeat this affirmation six to ten times. Each time, endeavor to feel the accomplishment as well. That is, feel or sense the emotion that this accomplishment will generate in you. Savor the feeling and enjoy it. If you are able to create pictures in your mind, imagine what your picture of success looks like and feel the thrill of accomplishing it. Your deeper mind resonates to, and acts on the combination of the feeling, the picture, and the words. All three produce in unison.

Once you have completed this anticipatory exercise, shift your attention to something completely different. By way of analogy, once you plant a seed it is important not to keep digging it up to check on its progress. You need to trust that your idea will take root and you need to nourish it with your good intentions and your affirmations.

The belief and faith that your inner mind can manifest your desires is critical to the success of the technique we have presented. It is easy, of course, to have faith in what is apparent, in what we have experienced and seen to be true. A new and different way of thinking is required to recognize that the invisible precedes the tangible. That the formless can create the form. This is the way and method of your deeper mind. Reflect carefully on this realization. Give it your full attention.

If you have a few spare moments during your day, you can reinforce your twilight zone work. Write out your affirmative statement and then say it aloud (or if this is not convenient, repeat silently to yourself). Visualize the desired outcome. Sense the good feeling of accomplishment you will be experiencing. Then resume your regular business duties.

This simple and powerful exercise we have described is designed to work in concert with your usual sales practices. You will likely find that, as a result of this "inner" work, your "outer" work will become more meaningful, satisfying, and effective. As you quietly persist with your mental and physical efforts, you will likely be amazed at your results.

You may feel like telling others about your magical methods and advising them to do likewise. However, for a number of sound reasons that go beyond the scope of this chapter, and perhaps beyond the scope of the normal thinking mind, we recommend that you keep this approach to yourself. Your responsibility is to fully develop your own capabilities. If others are meant to profit from the special insights and knowledge you now have at your disposal, they will discover these secrets on their own, just as you did. Expressed another way, when the student is ready the teacher will appear. Utilize your wisdom to your full advantage. Apply your new knowledge well.

To the extent you faithfully practice and believe in the power of your inner mind, you will experience far greater success and satisfaction.

4

Money Galore

In our sales coaching sessions, we are frequently asked if there is one easy, practical tip that can be utilized right away to increase business and bolster success. Indeed there is!

The application described in this chapter is so simple and straightforward that it is often overlooked or quickly dismissed. Without frequent encouragement and follow-up prompts, however, most people won't bother to apply this procedure, which takes a total of one minute per day.

At first glance what we are going to describe can sound outside the realm of probability. It may seem too fanciful and too far beyond normal reality. Fortunately, most top-performing salespeople are comfortable and excited about venturing into new territory.

You can give yourself an advantage over the competition if you are willing to temporality suspend judgment and just try out the recommended idea. Take this concept on a test run. Subject it to your own scrutiny. Implement it for a month and see if you experience worthwhile benefits. You will likely be very glad you kept an open mind and followed through.

The exercise does require that you continue with your normal sales activities. It is designed to synergistically complement your current efforts and make the most of what you bring to the table.

Here is the practice:

> Twice a day, for about thirty seconds, imagine yourself being showered by money.
>
> In your mind's eye, see large-currency bills falling all around you from the sky.
>
> Feel the excitement, heightened pleasure, and deep satisfaction that you would experience if this scene were really unfolding. Focus on feelings of abundance and joy.
>
> Resonate in this space for a few moments.
>
> Then resume your normal work activities. Direct your attention back to the job at hand.
>
> Be secure in the knowledge that good things are coming your way. Harbor a quiet and confident expectancy. Cultivate trust.

One of our sales clients told us about this marvelous little exercise twenty years ago. Since then, many of our clients have experimented with it. The results they have obtained have been consistent with guided visualization studies carried out at universities across the globe. This research has consistently shown that what we imagine being true, coupled with the emotion of experiencing it, tends to shape our perception of reality and the range of opportunities we recognize.

The simplicity of benefiting from imagery belies its complex and sophisticated nature. In a future chapter, we will look at some of the fascinating dynamics underlying its effectiveness and how to make the most of this resource. In the meantime, invoke the playfulness of your creative mind, suspending judgment and analysis for another day. Repeat the exercise daily for four weeks and then see where you are. You will have a sense of whether the endeavor has been worthwhile for you. You will know if you are enriched.

At your discretion, you can substitute a scenario of your own choosing in place of the money deluge. For example, you can see sales orders pouring in all around you, and the influx makes you feel wonderful! Some clients have imagined customers' checks floating down. They have reveled in a bubble of happiness.

Whether you visualize money, sales orders, or checks wafting down, invoke at least a couple of your senses. In your imagination, look around. What do you see? What do you hear? How does it make you feel? What would it be like to actually be there?

As you may have astutely recognized, your money torrent is a powerful metaphor for increased sales. It symbolizes enhanced prosperity and well-being. The technique you are using represents a concrete way of attuning your creative mind with new business avenues. You can realize more possibilities and follow-up on the ones having the most potential.

This deeper mind of yours always responds to your faithful and emotional input, shaping the nature of your next experience. Would you like more sales? Would you like money galore?

5

Elevate Your Sales Dialogue

Many top sales executives have emphasized the importance of having an engaging and productive business generating dialogue with their customers. What does this mean?

Starting with your own internal dialogue, describe yourself (to yourself) as someone who helps others. For example, you help people solve a problem they have. You help them satisfy a need, desire, or aspiration. Think of yourself as a "helper," rather than a "pitcher."

Right now, ask yourself, how can I be more helpful to my customers? What could you say, what could you do to be more helpful? Based on your industry experience, what are the common issues clients have? How can you best advise them? Begin to implement one of your recommendations. Professionals who elevate their sales dialogue report feeling more in charge of the sales process and more in harmony with their clients.

As you adopt this "helping" mentality and provide your customers with consistent, high-quality input aligned with their needs, you will be regarded as less of a salesperson and more of a trusted adviser. Building up genuine trust is a great investment in your sales future and will pay back significant dividends as your career progresses. You'll experience greater job satisfaction and make more money.

People everywhere have a fundamental need to be heard and understood. You build trust when you demonstrate that you understand what the client wants and suggest a good way of achieving his or her objective. The customer desires something and you provide the path to attaining it.

What the best in sales do today is to connect with people. Give individuals your full attention. Really look at them. Feel an alliance and endeavor to strengthen it. Clarify your customer's requirements. Discuss beneficial solutions.

Seasoned salespeople converse so easily. They use natural language that connects with others. When you listen to them, it doesn't sound like they are trying to sell. And in the traditional sense, they aren't. What they are doing is connecting with the buyers to understand their needs. With that comprehension, they can position and advance their product or service.

Focus on the degree of fit between what the client wants and what your product or service offers him or her. When, in the client's mind, there is a strong alignment between his or her requirements and what you are selling, the deal is ready to be closed. The client signals a readiness to move ahead. You can arrive there by being attentive, enthusiastic, and service-focused. Based on what you have learned about the customer, what could you say to him or her that would be helpful and appreciated? What aspect of the product could you comment on that would raise his or her enthusiasm for making the purchase?

Whatever you are selling, suggest two benefits linked to what the client has stated is important to him or her. Average salespeople mention one feature or benefit linked to client requirements—and, often, several more that have little to do with what the customer really wants.

Top-performing salespeople consistently make it a point to mention two attractive (to the customer) benefits.

You know well that buyers don't like to feel pressured. It's good for you to appreciate that in general, salespeople want to move forward more quickly than their prospects. While enthusiasm is commendable, it can also be what stands in the way of you closing a sale. It can be counterproductive. It can foster buying pressure. Most customers change their posture slightly when they feel forced or coerced. For example, some look down, some look away, and some look defensive. If you notice that a customer is becoming uncomfortable, what could you say to diffuse any tension?

Ask transparent questions, ones that will put the prospect back at ease.

Comfortably ask the customer if he or she would like something (of value to him or her). Depending on the context, ask:

- Would you like coffee?
- Would you like to browse?
- Would you like a test drive?
- Would you like more information?
- Would you like to schedule a follow-up meeting?
- Would you like to ask me some questions?
- Would you like to share your reservations with me?
- Would you like to move ahead?

There are challenges and temporary setbacks in any job or profession. If sales were easy, everybody would be lining up for your job. Sales is a specialty profession. It is both an art and a science. There's an art in being able to manage an engaging and compelling conversation.

There's a science to presenting your extensive product knowledge to perfectly match a client's needs.

To better align your intentions with your desired sales results, do this simple "mind reflection" technique one or two times daily, for about a minute each time. When you are alone, imagine you have just completed a sale. A customer has purchased from you. Hear yourself saying "Thank you." See yourself smiling in the mirror of your mind. Experience the feelings you would have if this were really happening. Feel the joy of success. Now resume your normal business activities. Make sure when you make the next sale that you say "thank you" and smile, just as you did in your imagination.

Your inner sales dialogue is as important as actual conversations with clients. You can project from the center of your mind to the circumference of your outer world. The greater your ability to internalize and actualize this core belief, the more success you will attain. Be sure to let yourself reflect with gladness on what you truly want then follow through with concrete actions to make this your reality.

Implementing one of the suggestions in this chapter will elevate the quality of your dualistic (internal and external) sales dialogue, leading to a more rewarding sales experience for you and your buyer.

6

Stay Upbeat

Enthusiasm sells. When you project excitement and satisfaction about your work, you are more easily able to persuade and influence others. Customers sense your upbeat disposition. They are likely to enjoy interacting with someone who is genuinely eager to assist them.

The face and personality you display to your customers needs to be sincere, otherwise clients will get the sense that you don't really care about them. If you act contrary to your true feelings, if you put on too much of a show or give an artificial pitch, you will squander your natural energy. You will give a measure of your vibrancy to each prospect and have nothing left for yourself.

Making slight, comfortable adjustments to your style is the better approach. You can effectively build on your solid foundation. To elevate your disposition, consciously dial up your enthusiasm by a notch.

In today's ultra-competitive, fast-paced world, it can be challenging to have clients experience the best that you have to offer. You can be most effective in your optimal state of mind.

25 SalesBoosters

Here are a few suggestions to help you to remain consistently enthusiastic across the diversity of your sales interactions. The following seven tips are simple and practical. You are likely doing most of these already. Perhaps there is one you know about but have not yet fully utilized.

1. Keep your internal dialogue—the conversation you have with yourself—positive and supportive. Your state of mind greatly affects how you feel and act. As you raise the quality of your inner talk, you subsequently elevate the caliber of your outward behavior.

2. Cultivate a hobby outside of work. This enjoyable activity will rejuvenate your mind and your passion for life. Look forward to fully immersing yourself in this endeavor at least once a week.

3. Periodically reward yourself for your work efforts. Behavior that is reinforced tends to be repeated, even at a subconscious level. Tangibly acknowledging your success is a great way to bolster your enthusiasm.

4. Practice "feeling good" more often. When you are stressed, frustrated, angry, or flat, recall a person or animal you love. Revel for a little while in this warm emotion. Raise the corners of your mouth in a tiny smile that stays with you. When you smile, you bring more sunshine into your life and into the lives of others.

5. Like the universe, people have a natural, inborn sense of wanting more. Rather than following the herd, consider carefully what you desire more of. Perhaps more prosperity? More wisdom? More peace of mind? Choose what is right and correct

for you. Chasing someone else's dream will ultimately contribute to feeling unfulfilled. Finding and following your own path will help to ensure you arrive at your desired destination.

6. Spend more time with uplifting people and less time with drainers. You have likely heard that you tend to get more of what you are focusing on. This expression is applicable at all levels of existence. Upbeat, forward-thinking people give rise to an inspirational frame of mind. Who inspires you?

7. This tip requires a mental transposition to a new viewpoint. Instead of "doing something" to maintain your edge, take little outward action to return to your natural state. This field of consciousness has been expressed as "grounding," "centering," and, most recently, as "mindfulness." You rediscover that you can have what you are seeking. There is great joy in being who you are, no more and no less. If you feel compelled to take action, catch an early sunrise. Walk in the (rain) forest. Observe a pretty flower. Stay still and listen. What is the message?

In your professional capacity, remaining at an ideal level of enthusiasm will benefit you and your customers. Top sellers minimize down periods and extend their resolve by better managing their moods. You can polarize yourself along the positive dimension by keeping these tips in mind. You will be less likely to be dragged down by others and more the master of your own world.

7

Close More Sales

Let's agree: Closing the sale is the point where your customer chooses to buy. They want what you are offering and are willing to pay for it. The purpose of interacting with clients is to obtain endorsement for moving ahead. If you invest time with a prospect and neglect to close the sale, you are the same distance from your goal as when you started. From a results perspective, closing is the most important aspect of the sales process.

In a recent qualitative study conducted by the author, fifty-six top sales producers provided recommendations on closing more sales. The advice they gave centered on three themes:

- Understand your customer
- Build trust
- Provide extra motivation

Our experts mentioned that while the close can be viewed as the definitive action step, good closing protocol begins with "hello" and concludes with "thank you." Keeping this perspective in mind, let's look at what our resilient pros recommend.

1. Understand your customer

Customers are more likely to buy from people who help them get what they want.

Janet, an appliance saleswoman, says the best way to close more sales is to ask straightforward questions to uncover the customer's wants and needs.

The customer says, *"I'm just comparison shopping today."* You comment, *"Well, that's an excellent approach. What features are most important for you to have? What price range best suits your budget?"*

"While treating the customer with friendly respect, identify what is key for them. Then match their requirements with your offerings. Simple, clear, and highly effective," comments Janet.

"My top salespeople are very good listeners," explains Terry, who manages a team of consumer electronics advisors. *"We ask, can I assist you in any way? Then, we respond according to what the customer says they want. We provide an environment where people feel comfortable. We treat people the way they want to be treated. Some demand lots of attention. Some don't. All buy. You need to listen well."*

Phil is one of the best real estate agents in Midwest Toronto. Last year, he led his branch in sales.

Be perfectly clear on what your client wants is his counsel. *"Help your buyer articulate their desires. At the beginning I inquire, what type of home are you looking for? What features do you want? What neighborhood amenities? After each showing, I ask, why would you be excited about living in this home? I confirm the buyer's preferences and feelings with them. Showing the right property closes the deal."*

Be more thoughtful and intentional with the questions you ask and their placement in your client dialogue.

2. **Build trust**

   Would you be more inclined to make a major purchase from a salesperson you trusted? Of course!

   Once a base level of trust is established, the buyer is inclined to favor that person or company. For a long time.

   Sarah sells high-fashion women's clothing. She says, *"I always endeavor to give my customers sound, helpful advice. I tell them what clothes compliment their features. I explain which outfits will look stunning on them. If something doesn't fit perfectly, I tell them and suggest a better alternative. My customers are assured I will help them look their best. They can depend on me. And they do."*

   As an automotive sales and leasing consultant, Mat's winning formula has been to operate with integrity. To be truthful, forthright, and helpful. To foster trust. To increase his clientele.

   "Our industry has had its share of hucksters," comments Mat. "Initially, customers tend to be on guard. I show them the numbers and explain how we sell at dealer invoice plus four percent. Added transportation and licensing fees are the *same as we pay. There are no hidden administrative costs, which almost all other dealerships tack on. Our transparent pricing causes customers to believe in us. Objections recede."*

– Connie is a successful female in the male-dominated securities industry, where one in three new advisers exit stage right after six months on the job. Yet Connie has prospered. *"What do people value in an investment adviser? Someone whose advice is tailored to his or her specific financial goals. I carefully assess their risk appetite and suggest what is best for them. Whether they buy or not, I update them on market trends and my recommendations. Over time they give me more of their portfolio."*

To what extent do you treat your customers the way you want to be treated?

3. Provide extra motivation

Shoppers may need a motivational push to make the purchase. They respond positively to an extra incentive to buy. This powerful technique is to be utilized at your discretion. It is a given that the incentive you are presenting is real and true. Sell always with integrity.

"Price is the most common objection I hear from clients," says bulk-packaging salesman Danny. *"If I don't close after my presentation, I'll endeavor to assess what else the client wants. Usually it's cost containment. For example, the purchasing agent moves to a 'yes' when I offer to include nine hundred extra free bags to complete our company production run. But only if they place the order today."*

Close More Sales

Gail told us how she utilizes a version of this technique in her door-to-door distributor business. *"When a woman buys—and eventually most do—I give them a couple of complimentary sample products. I may offer them a new cosmetic that just came out, no charge. My customers look forward to my visits. I love seeing them."*

Len leads the retail marketing of a high-quality camera line. Interested photographers are e-mailed a monthly shooting tip along with company news and updates, all viewable on one page. *"Prices are never discounted,"* says Len. *"The enticement is to own the finest camera in the world and to have the company's lifetime support in getting the most from it."*

What are two incentives you could offer that your customers would value?

You can appreciate that closing starts with your sales mind-set and your customer greeting. It's a perfect circle.

- *Ask questions so you know what your client wants.*
- *Build trust by operating with integrity.*
- *Create an extra incentive to buy.*

You will close more sales and do so enjoyably!

8

Say No to Rejection

Which salesperson has heard more refusals—the master or the novice?

By nature of their persistence and tenacity, seasoned performers have received more no's than have beginners. What separates the two groups is how they think about rejection. The experienced see rejection leading to greater success. New sellers view rejection as conclusive. To them, a no is final. It nixes the sale.

Professionals like you have a high need to be well regarded and well thought of. In psychological terms, this is called need for approval. Artists and athletes possess this attribute. In sales, this is a desirable qualification. It provides you with the drive and motivation to be successful. You want the purchaser to like you and your product enough to move ahead.

That being said, when you do your best to gain endorsement and the client refuses, it can be hard to accept. And yet, you also know that at some level, rejection is an essential part of the sales world.

Without rejection, without the opposite of winning the sale, there would be no reason for celebrating success. If sales just happened automatically, your resilience wouldn't be needed. Competition tends to bring out the best in people. Climbing the mountain is challenging, but the view from the top can be inspiring.

Considered from another perspective, if every day was sunny and the perfect temperature, after five months you would likely welcome rain. The cloudy interlude helps you better appreciate the nicer days. If you make every sale you work for, you may stop working. You may take your success too much for granted.

When a sale does not happen, there are four things to keep in mind. Internalizing these practices will help you say no to rejection.

1. You have heard this before: Let the feeling of being rejected dissipate on its own. Rather than taking it personally, recognize that occasional rejection goes with the territory. Are you professional enough to handle it constructively?

   Honor your feelings but don't dwell on them when you have more important things to do. It's psychologically healthy to acknowledge and accept your reactions to a situation or client. It's fine to be annoyed, disappointed, or angry for a short while. You can temporarily compartmentalize these feelings. After revisiting them a few times, let the emotion naturally fade away.

2. Consider what you did right with the prospect. Since a person tends to get more of what they focus on, recognizing what you did well will help you to demonstrate these behaviors in the future.

   What were you pleased with? Many people take their strengths and assets for granted. But discover this—are we not here in life and in our careers because of our strengths, because of the things we do well? Acknowledge to yourself what you did right. And for the time being, entertain only these positives.

3. Look for a bigger and more important message beyond the rejection. Ultimately, this could be worth far more than the sale you just lost.

    Ask yourself what you could have done better or differently. How can you apply your new learning toward making the next sale? Like the successful hunter, make your weaknesses your prey, subjecting them to the light of your better understanding. There is at least an iota of knowledge to be learned by rejection, even if it's to conclude that you did everything correctly. Sometimes a sale is just not meant to happen. Maybe the prospect was having a bad day and pushed everything helpful aside.

4. At your discretion, utilize the rejection response to better understand the customer's objections. Tell your prospect you welcome spontaneous feedback on the product or buying experience. You could then ask him or her some specific questions to identify reservations. For example:

    "Thank you for speaking with me. May I ask you two questions?"

    i. "How could this product better match your needs?"

    ii. "What would make you say yes today?"

    Depending on the situation, you may want to follow up with the person to see if he or she might change his or her mind. Occasionally customers do reconsider offers. No's are rarely permanent in the grander scheme of our continuum. There will be a time and a place when a no becomes a yes.

People who have done prospecting and cold calling for a while have learned to manage rejection productively. They understand there will be many no's before a sale is secured. They are mentally prepared to keep going. These individuals keep their focus on what they are doing now rather than being derailed by the past or enticed by the future. Each call is a new opportunity. They make the most of these by utilizing everything they have learned up to that point.

Could rejection ever be seen more clearly for what it is? It's simply a pause in the action. Have it work better for you!

9

Be Positively Negative

For every ten thoughts you have, how many are positive and constructive? What percentage of your inner conversation would be construed as negative? For the high-performing individuals, about 90 percent of their thinking is aligned with their stated goals. Ten percent is focused on concerns and potential setbacks. In many ways, this is the ideal balance between the opposite poles of thinking.

Numerous books have been written on the power of positive thinking. These excellent references state that what you think about, you tend to bring about. In other words, if you believe you will succeed, you will. And if you think you will fail, then you are probably right. Examined from a second perspective, the polarity of your state of mind galvanizes your world. If you cultivate a bright disposition, you will likely recognize more opportunities.

Thinking constructively is a great ally on your path to success. In moderation, so is negative thinking. Surprised? Let's examine why this is true and how you can use this obvious yet hidden insight to your advantage. You may experience newfound freedom along with the increased energy and vitality that accompany this realization. It's all good.

Psychologist's offices are full of people who have denied negative thoughts and emotions. People keep saying OK to things that aren't OK. They really want to say no. Instead, they tell themselves to be nice, to think kindly. It will all work out. Positive attitudes will prevail. Taken to the extreme, every obstacle becomes an opportunity to change or improve something. But a barrier by another name is a block. Figuratively, a gate is placed in your way so that you will pause and reflect.

It's better to vet negative feelings so that you can let go of them. Such an emotional release is healthier than denying or repressing how you feel. Acknowledging baser emotional states sheds new light on the origins of those reservations, concerns, and anxieties we all harbor.

Psychosomatic complaints and physical ailments can be brought about by suppressed emotions. Certain problems could be avoided if people would vent their feelings and stop dismissing them. This isn't about going on a rampage. It is just acknowledging one's own feelings and releasing them. One should always be honest with one's self.

Perhaps all we need to change is the way we view negativity. It is a fallacy to believe you should always think positively. There is nothing wrong with entertaining a few negative thoughts. When you know what you do not want, it helps you get clear on what you *do* want. Negative thinking serves as a reminder or cue to go deeper; to explore what is not quite right. And to resolve these issues. Clearly identifying what is wrong, you are enabled to objectively explore all options and possibilities.

When you have negative thoughts or reactions, think, "This is exactly how I should be feeling." Accept how you are now. Explore the reasons for feeling the way you do. Then you will feel better. Only when you accept and use the negative can you move to a more positive state. If you deny the negative, if you say "I shouldn't be feeling this way," it won't work. And when you try to override these feeling with positive ones, you will experience much resistance.

If you are sad and pretend to be happy, you become a victim of false thinking and behavior. You may end up not knowing who you truly are and be unable to move beyond a state of sadness, just going through the motions. This is self-delusional. You are unconsciously cheating yourself out of a richer, more vibrant life. Now aren't you glad that you are comfortable with the occasional cloud?

If you fail to make the sale and feel disappointed, experience that emotion for whatever duration and depth is right and correct for you. Embrace where you are. Clarify your intent. What do you want to achieve? What actions do you need to take to get there? Move forward when you are ready to—after you have utilized and worked through the negativity. After you have touched and grounded the negative energy.

If you are anxious or concerned about reaching your sales targets, explore the origins of these sensations. Face up to your feelings and get them out. Identify the root cause. Why do you feel this way? Once you have expressed yourself, figure out where you want to end up. Gradually begin formulating a solution to get to your desired outcome.

Sometime, you may find yourself saying "I don't feel very confident today." Acknowledge your transient disposition. Explore the reason why. Experience yourself more deeply. Ask yourself how you want to feel. Identify what you can do right now to bolster your belief in yourself.

Contrary to the idea that you should not put attention on negative things, the truth is, putting attention on the downside does not make it stronger if the intent is to work through your concerns. Once your reservations are visible (to yourself), you can draw on the full power of your resources to focus on what you desire.

You can more fully utilize your positive and negative feelings for the purposes they are meant to serve.

Choose the positive, but do not deny the negative. Recognize where you are then follow through to achieve what you want. Once in a while, be positively negative!

10

Restore Your Confidence

Even the most outwardly assured sales professionals have told us they would like to have more self-confidence. What would you do differently if you had all the confidence in the world?

Emily, a mortgage broker, told us she would be more influential with prospective clients, asking them for an exclusive two-day commitment while she identified the best financial provider for them.

Aerospace consultant Don remarked he would aggressively compete directly with larger firms, emphasizing to clients his impeccable record of delivering on time and on budget.

Morteza, who promotes India call center services to North American companies, said that, with sky-high belief in his capabilities, he would relax more with his clientele, better connecting with them while astutely listening to their service requirements.

Most representatives have indicated they would be appropriately bolder with an additional injection of self-confidence.

From a psychological perspective, confidence is reflected in two related qualities. First, self-confident people believe in their current capabilities—that is, the things they do well now. Occasionally remind yourself of your successes. Most often, these experiences have been enjoyable, too. When you recall these triumphs, experience again how they made you feel about yourself. When reflecting on self-confidence, stick to those instances where you performed well.

Second, self-confident people believe in their potential to improve—that is, to gradually acquire new skills, knowledge, and capabilities. By their nature, most salespeople are curious about life. They love to learn new things. People fascinate them. They want to learn everything they can about the products they sell.

If we have already learned everything we need to know, then our time has come and gone. Far better to have a thirst for more and to share in the wonder and excitement of life. If you recognize what you do well and are interested in continuous learning, you are on the right path toward becoming the person you want to be.

There are a variety of factors that can affect a person's self-confidence. How you feel about yourself tends to be reactionary, based on your past experiences. For example, say you've just signed six clients in a row. You're on top of the world and can hardly wait to interact with the next customer. Conversely, you've had a string of rejections and objections lately and you're not looking forward to seeing the next person, who will surely also be difficult.

It's as normal to have periods when you feel the world is your oyster as it is to have times of self-doubt. The principle of rhythm dictates that just like the tides, seasons, and the economy, everyone will experience ebb and flow.

When your confidence is less than you would like it to be, there is a wonderful exercise you can use to get back on track. This little gem is called the Mirror Technique.

Restore Your Confidence

The Mirror Technique has been used by thousands of sales professionals to give them an automatic boost in confidence and presence. Claude Bristol first presented this great esteem builder in his bestselling classic *The Magic of Believing*, published back in 1948. We updated his excellent recommendation, first in 1987, and again in 2014, based on our coaching experience with sales professionals.

To strengthen belief in yourself, proceed as follows:

- Stand in front of a mirror so that you can clearly look into your own eyes.

- Take two easy, relaxing breaths.

- Now look intently into your eyes, sensing that you are connecting with the deepest level of your consciousness, your true self.

- While maintaining your inward focus, slowly and firmly say to yourself in a low voice: "I am calm, relaxed, and confident in all situations and circumstances. People believe in me because I believe in myself."

- Repeat a few times daily, when you have a chance to do so. This could easily be any time you look in a mirror.

This is truly an amazing technique that you should try out for yourself. As we have discussed previously, there is a sizable difference between understanding this exercise intellectually and realizing the benefits. To prosper from your new knowledge, you need to apply it practically. You need to employ the Mirror Technique. Then, based on the improvements you gain, the new knowledge becomes your truth.

As with all self-improvement endeavors, we recommend keeping your associated actions to yourself, for yourself. Expressed another way, never allow anyone a view into your inner sanctuary. Let results and your persuasive personality speak for you.

Resilient self-confidence is one of the most essential traits for salespeople to possess and draw upon. When you believe in yourself, the world believes in you, too.

11

Sharpen Your Focus

You tend to get more of what you focus on.

This statement explains much about how our thinking affects the reality we experience. As we fix our attention on something, the subject of our concentration becomes prominent. It occupies more of our consciousness.

From a practical perspective, thinking about finding a solution to a problem usually leads to identifying helpful approaches. For example, Sabrina wants to bring in more sales. When she is not meeting with clients, she considers ways to generate new business. Useful ideas pop into her mind, often when she is pruning her home garden.

Conversely, ruminating too much on dissatisfactions can turn a setback into a larger obstacle than it really is. Alfred says he wants additional customers. He thinks it will be very challenging to fulfill his wish, given the market he sees. Every day, he notes more negative news in the paper, confirming his suspicions that things are difficult. Alfred complains to his friends about the deteriorating condition of the economy.

Over the coming weeks, which person will identify more prospects? Sabrina is looking for new opportunities and will likely find some.

Alfred has been expanding and reinforcing his resistance proposition. He anticipates insurmountable barriers along with negligible results. Alfred doesn't bother to work smarter, as he already knows he won't make his quarter numbers. New customers elude him.

It's worth taking a step back periodically to see where our thinking has taken us. The circumstances we are presently in have a lot to do with the thoughts we hold dear. Do you see the connection?

Many people defeat themselves, without realizing what they are doing or intending to, in little ways that add up. Metaphorically speaking, you are free to tinge your perceptions with whatever color you choose. What is important is to consciously select the shade that is right for you.

Our statement "you tend to get more of what you focus on," also implies that if you shift your attention, you can alter the state of your circumstances. This means you still need to take action and follow through, but you will be working in concert with your intentions. Getting results is significantly harder if you are fighting yourself.

When you zero in on what you are doing, you can draw on the full power of your resources. Like the sun's rays that are concentrated by a magnifying glass, your attention is directed like a laser. Your resources are ignited. The sum total of what you have learned thus far is considerable as you discover new ideas, approaches, and possibilities.

Does it make sense for you to be more in control of your thinking and reasoning processes? If not, who is—advertisers? The company you keep? Whatever impinges on your consciousness? In the extreme, a person's focus can be so scattered and transient that they are jumping from one thing to the next, not really taking much in. They are a pawn, rather than a player, in the game of life.

As you move through your professional day, focus your attention more on what you are doing and less on extraneous thoughts. Mind your own business! That is, pay attention to, and advance your priorities. Use your thinking and reasoning processes to achieve your goals. Make sure that your thoughts are aligned with your intentions. When your mind wanders excessively, gently redirect it back on what you are doing. If you like, you can immediately neutralize and render ineffective any extraneous thoughts by silently saying the words, "Cancel, cancel."

Before taking action, remind yourself of your intent, what you want to achieve. While keeping your overall objective in mind, successively focus on the components that will get your there. In sales, for example, your intent may be to have a wonderful client meeting that will lead to new business. Direct your focus on interacting successfully with your customer rather than on the outcome of the sale. In the field, keep your focus on the constituents who will lead to the sale rather than on the sale itself.

It's important to mention that there is nothing wrong with negative thinking, especially if the intention is to understand what went wrong in order to fix a problem. At the same time, you should recognize that too much negativity is likely to produce more negativity and serve only to reinforce a preexisting state of mind. Just be aware that what you are planting in your consciousness takes root in your world. A few weeds are OK, even desirable under some circumstances. But too many can choke the flowers.

Have you observed that many people go through life reasonably content with the status quo of their existence? They don't give much thought to where they place their attention. For them, thinking is just something that happens. As we have seen, their habitual patterns of thought may be undermining their success, without them even being aware of it.

Highly successful people recognize that the best way to create the future they desire is by managing their present moments well. If you are to operate at an enhanced level, pay more attention to what you are focusing on. Ensure your thinking is moving you toward your goals. When you sharpen your focus, you accentuate your sales.

12

Walk This Way

Have you noticed that highly confident people radiate a presence that expands beyond physical stature? A highly confident person walks into a crowded restaurant and is noticed. There is something special about him or her that draws in others. In sales, confidence is a great asset.

It's worth examining how confidence and ego differ. We have all met individuals who are legends in their own minds. Full of self-importance, these people take themselves and the success they have achieved far too seriously. They crave attention but don't want to give much back.

Truly confident professionals feel a strong sense of gratitude for their wins. They are clear on what they want to accomplish. They believe they will be able to continue to progress toward their objectives. These sales titans focus more on others than on themselves. Through giving to customers, they help themselves. Confident people give in greater proportion than they expect to receive in return.

Self-assured salespeople provide their customers with a sense of increase. People enjoy interacting with them. Clients are enriched by the attentive, courteous, and helpful advice they receive. Customers feel valued. They are sure they made the right choice. Their purchase fills a missing void. High confidence is top salesmanship.

Is there a self-development area where you would like to exhibit greater confidence? Even outstanding sales producers respond yes to this query. There is always a situation or circumstance that could be better faced with a boost in confidence.

When you think about being in a sales dialogue, visualize yourself as the person you desire to be. Picture yourself as slightly more self-assured that you are now. The apparent simplicity of this cognitive technique belies its effectiveness. But when you engage in self-reflection you realize you are largely the person you believe yourself to be. And as you incrementally shift your image of yourself you unshackle more of your potential.

Make it a mental habit to strengthen the confidence you possess in your mind's eye. Stretch it just a little bit. Keep gently pushing yourself upward. Membership is lifetime. Your supportive and gradual improvements will be amply rewarded.

In the meantime, here are a few quick tips that will help you become the professional you have in mind. Choose one and get started right away.

- **Dress Sharper.** When you feel good about your appearance, you are more likely to exude confidence. Does your appearance reflect the winner you see in the mirror?
- **Walk Taller.** Leaders can appear taller than they actually are. If you felt taller, could you project yourself better?
- **Feel Gratitude.** Being thankful for where you have arrived establishes greater receptivity for new opportunities. Are you appreciative of what you have now?

- **Compliment Others**. People resonate with sincere acknowledgments. Did you compliment someone today?

Steady advancements in how you feel about yourself and your ability to create the future you want through managing your present moments well will produce many favorable outcomes over time. Can you walk this way often? Most assuredly!

13

Find Career Joy

"I always want to be selling," said Fred. *"My parents are in sales and I think there's a genetic connection. For me, having something to sell that I can get excited about, along with unlimited earning potential, is very motivating."*

Amanda commented, "Each day, I want to enjoy what I'm doing and finish up with a sense of professional fulfillment and satisfaction. I need to believe in my product. I think my philosophy is about outworking the competition, having fun, and making money."

Christine added, "My goal is to coach and lead the team. I'm one of seven reps now. Within a two-year window, I aspire to move up to a sales management position. For me, ultimate success is selling each salesperson on themselves."

Mat told us, "Giving financial advice to clients makes me feel good. I like the combination of providing unconditional guidance and selling tailored products."

How you feel about your work will, of course, affect your longer-term sales performance. To the extent you are doing what you enjoy, you will experience a good deal of career satisfaction. Conversely, the greater the gap between your job duties and your true interests the more you will feel dissatisfied and unmotivated.

In the extreme, continued career dissatisfaction can produce general apathy and malaise. A person is just going through the motions, putting in his or her time as a working stiff. He or she may be letting others temporarily dictate routine. Under these circumstances an individual might find him- or herself looking to regain a sense of vocational adventure and a zest for life.

There are two crucial questions that must be considered integral with top-tier career engagement. You could spend a week identifying and analyzing your vocational talents and potential. While this endeavor is all well and good, true happiness with your job always comes back to these clusters:

1. What are you naturally good at?
2. What do you most enjoy doing?

When you are able to do what fits you well, you can excel in good times and hold your own in bad. You can also easily tough it out with less-than-desirable bosses, companies, and conditions, often outlasting them and moving on to more ideal settings.

If you are stuck with a daily grind that's out of sync with who you are, life becomes a constant struggle that gradually dims your inner glow. Fortunately, you can kindle your sales passion and find career joy.

To rediscover what you are naturally good at, visit your collection of childhood memories. Thinking back, identify what was effortless for you.

Fred remembered his paper route and the thrill he felt signing up new customers. *"I just asked them if they would please count on me to deliver their morning paper, inside their screen door, rain or shine, every morning. Most people said yes."*

"We competed with kids down the street selling lemonade in the hot summer months," said Amanda. *"I spent hours in the garage making the best stand in the neighborhood. Up and running, it felt like a party. We had music from my mother's borrowed transistor radio. I loved attracting the traffic and the attention we got."*

What comes easily to you reflects your innate abilities. Question number one (above) examines these comfortable traits and skills. They are an expression of who you are. And when you can just be yourself, there's a wonderful flow to life and an encouraging connection with all that is.

Our second query (what you most enjoy doing) focuses on your interests. As you do what you like, you are continuously rejuvenated. Each sales interaction is new and fresh.

"When I can trade a person's long face for a smile, that's what I really like to see," commented Christine. *"I enjoy raising the group's disposition and energy level. I look forward to helping our team. I feel a bond with my colleagues."*

"I've always felt good giving people advice. First comes the guidance based on what is best for the client. Then, with the right aligned product, the buy in agreement is seamless. This type of selling is so rewarding on multiple levels," Mat said.

Periodically ask yourself what you are naturally good at. Record your answer.

Reflect on what you most enjoy doing. Write up your insight.

Notice how these simple yet effective questions illuminate your job abilities and your vocational interests, respectively. Either will steer you toward the future you desire.

For most salespeople, there is a good deal of overlap between their abilities and interests. They are concentric circles. Where they intersect is career joy. Identify this area and see where you stand. Then put your findings to work for you!

14

Raise Your Energy

Feeling drained?

At some point, everyone obviously says yes to this question. Long work hours, stressful situations, family obligations, lack of sleep, as well as a host of other factors can tax our stamina.

For the sales professional, having good energy is paramount to influencing customers and galvanizing them toward action. Energy that's focused and directed is a powerful ally in achieving your targets.

The next time you are feeling depleted, try out the following visualization technique. Originally developed by Stirling University professor Ronald Shone in 1984, it has been used by hundreds of account managers and reps to help them quickly perk up. It has helped these people regain good feelings, confidence, and enthusiasm for life. We updated the exercise in 2014 based on our practice research. You will find the exercise speaks for itself through the feelings it produces in you. Review the approach a few times prior to trying it out yourself.

After you have done the exercise and feel familiar with it, read and reflect on the subsequent comments provided. These will give you a deeper understanding of the procedure, content and architecture.

The technique is deceptively (but positively) simple; much thought has gone into it.

> Begin by imagining that you are lying comfortably on a bed or couch. Your eyes are closed. Pretend you are very relaxed. You fall asleep quickly and begin to dream. The dream seems very real to you, so real that you briefly wonder whether you are awake or asleep, or in-between.
>
> In your dream, a beam of sunlight comes down and envelops your whole body. See yourself bathed in golden light.
>
> You travel up the beam and go close to the sun. As you approach, you are infused with wonderful energy. You can feel your cheeks glowing. This sensation spreads throughout your body.
>
> Your entire being begins to radiate this life source. With each breath you take, you inhale more sunshine. Every cell, organ, and system in your body becomes alive with energy.
>
> When you are ready, you return along the same beam of light that brought you there. You wake up fully, opening your eyes. You stand, feeling energetic and ready to go.

Only do this exercise when you can safely give it your full attention. After you have utilized the exercise eight or more times, you can leave your eyes open if you choose.

You can go as close to the sun as you want. Some people like to imagine they are on, or in, the sun. You can wear clothing or not.

When utilizing this approach, it is quite sufficient to imagine you are very relaxed. It's not necessary for you to go through a progressive relaxation or countdown sequence.

If you like, you can repeat an affirmation while you are with the sun. For example, you could say: "Every cell of my body is now being energized."

Advanced practitioners can utilize this exercise for other benefits. You could imagine the sunshine is healing you. Or you could feel that each ray of sunshine brings about a new sales opportunity.

As with all inner improvement endeavors, keep this path to yourself. Talking about it to other people can put you off track and undermine progress. Allow individuals to discover what is right for them. Mind your own business—meaning, look after your storefront and customers!

Return to the sun as you wish.

15

Mend Relationships

Here is a useful and effective way to easily deal with difficult customers, bosses, or colleagues who won't go away. Or perhaps they do, only to be replaced by even worse substitutes. If it's inadvisable to confront, rebuff, or drop these people, you can use the high-level tip in this chapter to transform your interactions.

Do try conventional means first. Summon your best efforts to win the adversary over. Be kind. Genuinely try to help the person. Allow him or her to experience the best of you. If your peerless relationship building efforts fall short, and you witness no improvement, let us explain how you can implement your mental powers to tip the scales in your favor.

This is an abstract concept that will require a shift in your usual thinking pattern. The highest level of mind, called the superconscious, is associated with all that is good. Your spirit, your essence, resides here. Generosity, unconditional goodwill, and feelings of benevolence are integral to the superconscious. Your superconscious is not bound by time and space conditions. You can project it wherever you wish.

Access to the superconscious is made using your conscious mind and choosing to direct your attention in a certain direction. The subconscious comes into play as well, by invoking images and feelings associated with what you are consciously thinking about. All you need to remember is that the three levels of mind operate in unison to amplify your true intentions.

While you are seemingly calling on the powers of your imagination, the results you achieve will be real.

For this exercise to be successful—which it will be—you need to possess a good imagination. You need to entertain possibilities that would be quickly and erroneously dismissed by the average person. As you are into sales, and as sales is in you, too, your capacity for considering the metaphysical is right where it needs to be to produce maximum results.

> When you are in a quiet place, think of the person you desire to have a better relationship with. Now imagine that your highest level of mind is connecting with theirs. Allow your high mind to welcome the other person's high mind. Be comfortable in this mode for about thirty seconds or so, several times a day, or whenever you think about the individual.

With permission, we selected a few examples from our client files to illustrate how the process can work for you.

"'Detest' is a strong word but it sums up how we felt about working with that woman. All the girls in the department avoided her as much as possible. I thought about our high minds connecting and had an image of two hearts beating together. Over time, she began to treat me better than the rest. She recommended me for a team leader position and I moved on to a great boss and mentor."

"I dreaded having to deal with this particular client. As relationship manager, I had to endure his negative attitude and surly demeanor. No

matter how much preparation I did, I left his office feeling agitated. My usual confidence would evaporate. When I did the superconscious exercise, I experienced a profound sense of calmness and peace. I was freed from the control he had over me. Now I can patiently listen to his jaded perspective and offer my opinions based on research and facts. I'm not taking this codger's attacks personally. It's liberating."

"*'Tony the Terrible' targeted broker's assistants and entry-level newbies, calling them out publicly when they fell short on their quotas. He delighted in these tongue lashings and I hated him for it. As instructed, I thought about my superconscious and projected it next to his. I never got to liking him but the exercise helped me to feel comfortable with myself in his presence. Tony was eventually fired, which produced broad grins on everyone's faces. Mine was not out of malice but out of my personal victory. I won over the situation.*"

"I did the exercise as described a couple of times and felt better. On the third occasion, I had a great insight—that people act the way they do because they can't be any other way in that moment. We are conditioned and programmed to be as we are. Rather than judge, blame, or criticize, I decided to be more of a neutral observer, and to connect with the person in a new, invisible way. This has helped a lot."

To capture the essence of this exercise, the most frequent comment we have heard from sales professionals is that it has detached them from the drama of dysfunctional relationships. What would that be worth to you? Try it and see for yourself.

16

Eight Ways to "New"

People are naturally inquisitive. They are drawn to those things they haven't seen or experienced before, especially in relation to their interests. Customers will often buy new products and services just to be the first to try them out. Think about what this interesting human trait and resulting consumer behavior means to you and your business proposition.

If two brands of chewing gum have equal market share and one announces enhanced flavor, it will usually outsell the competition in the month it's introduced. A redesigned lottery game that offers increased odds of winning will be well received by gamers. Skin creams that contain recently discovered rejuvenating emollients are always popular. "New and improved" tends to get our attention and capture our imagination. By extension, when customers picture themselves happily using the fresh offering, the sale is mostly made.

Ask yourself, what's new about me? Are you excited about where you are headed? Retaining your spark, your motivation, and your zest for life will help you stay engaged with, and optimistic about, the future. You will be contemporary.

There are many ways to say yes to life, from your style and outlook to the products and services you represent. The eight prescriptions

25 SalesBoosters

below for remaining in vogue have been utilized with great success by our clients. One of these may be right for you.

1. **Look sharp.** Each day, give attention to your professional appearance. Periodically incorporate something that is new. You will radiate a presence that is appealing.
2. **Employ mentalism.** The physical actions you take, such as approaching customers, clarifying needs, listening, presenting benefits, and asking for the sale, are integral to your prosperity. To maximize your potential, continue to develop your powers of creative visualization by constructively using imagery and other mental techniques. For example, take a minute to feel the thrill, excitement and satisfaction of seeing (in your mind) new orders coming in. Or attract new customers by being grateful for the ones you have assisted already. Your state of mind is just as important as your product knowledge and selling skills.
3. **Show enthusiasm.** We have referenced this previously—emotional states are contagious. Look for ways to believe in yourself and your product to greater degrees. Remind yourself by saying, "My products are excellent—people believe in me because I believe in myself."
4. **Be client-focused.** Make your clients feel special and exciting. Develop a small arsenal of interesting questions focused on them that will better absorb them into the sales experience. Continually come up with comfortable yet intriguing inquiries and comments. Can you move past "How are you today?"
5. **Bolster your product knowledge.** The more you know about your product, the greater your potential for providing your customers with useful, helpful information that will influence their buying decisions. Become an expert on what you are selling. Be able to articulate what is new, improved, and exciting about it, particularly as is relates to your customer's narrative (how they want their world to be).

6. **Study the competition.** Does your company have 100 percent of the market? Pay attention to what your competitors are doing that keeps them in business. By definition, they must be meeting at least some customer's needs. Analyzing what others are doing well, and incorporating what you have learned, can help you elevate your game. What could you do better?
7. **Note global trends.** Look beyond your business segment and across other markets to identify new developments. To the extent you can establish a link or an association between what you are selling and what is happening globally, your product will become more relevant to the customer. For example, the capacitors you are selling to a domestic electronics company are made in a Taiwan factory that has recently earned the highest level of ISO certification. Top quality, reliability, and durability are the hallmarks of your purchaser. What a great fit!
8. **Master technology.** This means utilizing it in the best way for you. While shadowing the latest digital advances is all well and good, this will not separate you from the herd in business networking and online sales. The web offers wonderful marketing opportunities and unprecedented growth potential for those who can set themselves up—and sufficiently apart—from others. Ask customers what would make them come back to your site. Routinely think about how your media presence can drive more sales. Is it working?

Day in and day out, we are either advancing in our craft or sliding back. The "same-old" will get us nowhere close to our aspirations. Selectively implementing one or two of the tips mentioned will ensure you stay on the path of continuous improvement and in demand with your customers. Sales is a wonderful profession, and we are fortunate to be evolving with it.

17

Copy Right

Who do you most admire for their selling skills? The clients we work with usually mention another sales professional they look up to, someone whose expertise they would like to eventually acquire. It's great to have people in our physical, textual, or virtual environment we can profit from.

Here's a nifty technique we have utilized with good effect. It can speed up your learning curve and increase your achievement motivation. It will help you strengthen your sales profile—and the entire exercise takes less than five minutes. You need a quiet space where you can focus on your inner world without being disturbed or interrupted. Sit in a comfortable position.

> Begin the protocol with a specific intent to elevate one of your existing sales capabilities. Or select one you would like to have but presently lack. For example, maybe you aspire to better connect with clients such that they are drawn to you and comfortably tell you what they are seeking. Or perhaps you aim to demonstrate more persuasive and influential closing skills.
>
> In your mind identify a suitable role model or mentor, one who exemplifies the trait or skill you wish to have. This person

may be someone you know well or someone you have read about or seen speak at a conference. In addition, you need to harbor positive feelings about the person you've chosen, make sure it's someone you like and respect.

Have someone clearly in view? Now close your eyes and imagine this person is across from you. Feel his or her presence close by. Visualize the person demonstrating the exact skill you have referenced. Hear what he or she is saying. See and understand how he or she is proceeding. Take in everything the person is doing. Totally absorb this learning experience.

Ask the person if he or she will help you with your improvement efforts. Wait for the person to say yes or to smile and nod affirmatively. Imagine your sponsor changing into a six-inch-tall column or beam of white, radiant light. See this energy moving toward you. It enters your body at the top of your head and slowly descends to your heart. Filling your heart, it infuses every cell of this central organ. Imagine this as best as you can. Confirm to yourself that you welcome this expertise. Sense that new thoughts and new behaviors will be manifested with customers.

To complete the skill trance fusion, say "Thank you," three times, slowly and with deliberate gratitude. When you are ready, open your eyes and resume your activities.

Most of our clients have reported tangible benefits after just one application of this exercise. It's easy and simple to do, and over time, a great way to bolster your other improvement efforts.

There are a few points we would like to emphasize. They are the same things we would say if we were meeting with you in person.

Like many of the techniques we present for your benefit, this one is deceptively simple yet powerful and effective.

It is important to follow the instructions exactly and not add modifications or substitutions. Believe wholeheartedly in your potential and in your upcoming prosperity.

Practice at times when you can devote your full attention to the endeavor. And, of course, avoid doing this exercise when you are driving, operating equipment, or performing other tasks.

Rather than describing or discussing the exercise with colleagues, let them decide if it is right for them. As with the other exercises in this book, keep this one to yourself and evaluate its merits based on your own efforts and successes. One day soon, a few select colleagues will be copying the gift of your affluence.

18

The Five Whys

Japanese-produced goods, renowned for their quality, are based on peerless manufacturing and a continuous improvement philosophy. When a component fails in durability testing, in-house associates ask why the part broke. Often unsatisfied with the first reason, they keep looking until they arrive at the underlying root cause.

1. Why did the water pump fail? The seal started to leak.
2. Why did the seal leak? The bearing inside went bad.
3. Why did the bearing go south? The bearing retaining cage broke.
4. Why did the bearing cage break? The balls inside seized.
5. Why did the balls seize? They were insufficiently hardened.

In this case, the primary reason for the water pump failure was identified. By persisting with the "why" line of questioning, the true source of the problem was uncovered. This approach, as practiced by engineers and scientists, is also an illuminating, helpful sales diagnostic that can be utilized to understand what's behind the first, second or third anomaly. The initial answer to the "why" question usually masks a deeper cause. Rarely will you need to go beyond four or five inquiries to uncover the precursor.

Let's look at a sales-related example:

1. Why did I lose the RFP bid? I guess the other company was better.
2. Why was the other firm superior? The reps gave a more convincing presentation.
3. Why was their presentation more persuasive? What they said resonated with the client.
4. Why did the corporate prospect respond so positively to the competitor's pitch? Because they proposed an innovative solution the client thought was better aligned with the company's new marketing direction.

In this instance, the sales professional was able to see beyond the competitor's convincing presentation to appreciate that his or her rival better grasped the buyers evolving needs and tailored an argument to suit. This understanding will help the salesperson in his or her next RFP submission. The salesperson will likely do greater upfront probing and research, testing and verifying the approach with the buyer.

It's easy to quickly accept an obvious yet superficial explanation why your client didn't buy from you. You know that price is often cited as an objection, but is this the complete reason? There may well be a reservation or two lurking beyond the stated rejection. Most salespeople ask "why" just once. This is a good beginning, but not the whole story. Probing deeper will give you an advantage.

We recommend staying with the "why" line of questioning rather than substituting another word or phrase, such as "when," "what," or "how." These alternative paths are often longer, more circuitous, and more complicated than the more direct route. A little work is required to keep framing progressively more targeted "why" questions. Review

The Five Whys

the provided examples a few times and you will quickly get the hang of it.

It's a great idea to occasionally review your successes and identify the key feelings, beliefs, and actions that contribute to your sales victories. When you take this direction, the five "whys" can highlight core capabilities that you underestimate or take for granted. You may want to rely on these assets to a greater extent.

1. Why did I make that sale? I felt confident and assured.
2. Why was I feeling so capable? I was having a day when I was at the top of my game.
3. Why was I at the top of my game? The day just started out well and kept going.
4. Why did the day get off to a good start? I woke up with a positive, constructive orientation.
5. Why did I have a winning disposition? I began with an enabling frame of mind, believing in myself and in my product.

In this instance, our sales executive reminded herself that her greatest ally is her power of thought. We can express this in words by saying right thinking leads to right action; and right action benefits all.

Take a moment now and ask yourself, why, professionally speaking, you have achieved your current level of success. Ask three to five subsequent "why" questions. With each answer, probe a little deeper. Identify the basis of your well-being. Appreciate it as a source of prosperity for you.

Pursing the five whys line of questioning can be particularly helpful when you experience an outcome that surprises you. Maybe you expected to get the sale and you lost it. Or, your customer quickly says yes when you thought he or she would raise significant reservations. The five whys can provide you with greater self-awareness. This practical insight will help you sharpen your game. Take a close look at who you are, and who you are in the process of becoming. Why are you this way?

Of course, there are other interesting and practical uses of the five whys technique:

You can employ it to better understand your feelings and emotions.
- I am stressed. Why?
- I feel wonderfully relaxed and at ease. Why?

You can ask to understand great spiritual precepts.
- I am alive. Why?
- The Emerald Tablet cryptically declares: "As above, so below." Why?

It may take a while for deeper answers to become apparent. Be patient and supportive of yourself. As you genuinely seek an answer, it will arrive.

Let the five whys unlock the truth for you.

19

First Calls

Motivational speakers—those who give talks and sell ideas—spend hours preparing and rehearsing their presentations. In addition to becoming subject matter experts, they learn ways to captivate their audience. They provide people with good reasons to keep listening. Seasoned presenters often preview attendees' demographics so they can better tailor seminar content to the individual's needs. Should you follow suit?

Corporate buyers indicate that more than half of the salespeople who call or e-mail them for an initial introductory meeting are largely unprepared.

Al, a senior procurement officer for IT solutions at a financial services organization relates: *"I need to be given a convincing reason why I should meet with the prospector. What separates those who get in the door from those left on the sidewalk is their level of preparation."*

Amara, a strategic sourcing officer with a global hotel chain, concurs. *"Everyone wants an appointment to see us but only one in twenty earn the right to meet. The successful reps do their homework."*

Many potential opportunities are wasted through lack of proper preliminary background work. If you agree that preparing for that first call is critical, why do you suppose so many of your peers rely too heavily on their persuasive skills? It's not laziness or lack of drive. More likely, it's simply that action-oriented and achievement-focused people possess a strong desire to be out in the field selling. Once they realize that spending extra time properly preparing for the call will help them land more business, they will be more open to upfront review.

Often, your relationship with a new client begins with your pre-call analysis. Here are a few sample questions to consider prior to reaching out to future purchasers:

- Who is the best person in the company to contact?
- What would compel the contact to meet with me?
- Why is the buyer purchasing a product or service from someone else?
- When I connect, what can I offer that has a unique angle?

These days, it's also easy to research the person you are contacting on LinkedIn or an equivalent site. Sketch a profile of the individual, noting information that will help you make a better call. Is there a common interest you can selectively bring up at the right time? From the social media data, what can you deduce about the person's thinking style? Is he or she analytical, creative, practical, intuitive? What type of pre-meeting presentation will he or she best respond to?

You will also want to research the industry, noting new trends and developments. Where does the company fit in its market? Is it leading-edge? Is it a niche player? What does the company stand for? What does it aspire to? How can your product or service help the company solve a pressing need?

Assess the competition. In our experience, reps tend to know too little about who is across the street. The more you understand about your rivals' strengths and gaps, the better you can determine how right your product or service is for the customer. The other salesperson's constraints can represent a service opportunity for you that you can float in the pre-visit: *"I'd just like to mention that our product is packaged with no-charge automatic updates perpetually. Would this be of interest to you? During our meeting, I'll show how it can benefit your organization. The savings and convenience for you will be substantial over time."*

Doing mundane background work will be easier and more satisfying as it begins to pay off. Experiment with different levels of preparation, from what you are doing now to more in-depth review. Then decide if your want to make it an integral component of your planning process.

Let's also recognize that there are sales scenarios where it's not feasible to do traditional background research on the person you are meeting with. For example, you find yourself sitting on a plane beside a potential client. Or, you are introduced to a prospect at a golf tournament. We recommend you stick with social conversation until the other person specifically asks about your work activities. As things wind down, you can then indicate you would be pleased to help him or her and, if he or she would like, you will schedule a call. When in a social context, leave the person eagerly wanting additional product information. That way, he or she will be more open to meeting professionally with you.

Rather than being forceful, let things unfold as they will. Both of these expressions are true: The early bird gets the worm. The second mouse gets the cheese. While its excellent being first out of the gate, there is also great merit in timing your successes. Expressed another way, occasionally a studied approach is called for. Do what feels instinctively right at the time. When you get the go-ahead to connect, be fully prepared.

Perhaps you already have 100 percent of the market and can rightfully continue with what has worked so well for you. If there is an opportunity to bring in additional business, doing more deliberate preparation will help you get your foot in the door more frequently. Then you'll be all set to go forward with the sale.

20

Take Action

In your professional life, what are you putting off or avoiding? How important is this activity for your success? Procrastinating on tasks of minor significance can represent good time utilization, especially when your focus is on addressing high-impact items. Continually deferring till tomorrow what needs to be accomplished today, however, can compromise your drive and eventually cost you the sale.

There are three primary reasons that prevent people from initiating action. The main barriers to following through are fear, uncertainty, and lethargy.

> Annie was afraid to present to a difficult, challenging client. On a joint call with a male colleague, she had witnessed this woman shooting down her peer's comments, negatively questioning his pension product. *"I don't want to see her,"* Annie said.
>
> Arnold felt stuck. He wanted the sale, but didn't know the best way to proceed. His customer was giving buying signals but wanted a price concession. The sales manager said: *"Sell this exclusive vehicle at full retail, no deals."* Arnold wondered, what do I do next?

Stephen couldn't seem to get going. Discouraged with the previous day's lack of results cold-calling for appointments, he didn't feel like picking up the phone and starting again. *"I'm not up for the job,"* Stephen reflected.

As you have found yourself in similar scenarios, you know the way forward is to understand and accept the situation you are in and then address it. You have also likely discovered, as we have, that it's often quite sufficient to just improve the surrounding conditions. Some dilemmas just cannot be fully rectified or perfectly solved—but most can be smoothed over and refined.

There is a simple two-step process that has proven effective in these types of predicaments. First, begin by identifying what is holding you back. Then ask yourself what one action you can take to move yourself forward.

To illustrate, Annie quickly identified her fear of being rejected by domineering, outwardly hostile individuals. When she thought about the potential confrontation, she decided to play out her fear. She would pretend while meeting with the cantankerous buyer that she was acting in a dramatic play, relaxed and confident. Annie loved being in amateur theater, and she began to feel, in her altered state of mind, that she could calmly respond to the woman's attacks. The in-person meeting went well. Annie was patient, kind, and professional, exactly like she imagined she would be. She secured the account.

Implementing our advice, Arnold understood that he was caught between a customer's desires and his company's policies. The action he took was to be transparent with his client, advising the client that he would like to come down in price but that he simply had no leeway on such a limited vehicle. He also pitched several advantages of his dealership that went beyond costs. The customer passed, but

Take Action

Arnold was pleased that he had endeavored to close the sale, both by emphasizing the exclusivity of the vehicle and by promoting his company's customer-care etiquette.

Stephen acknowledged his lack of drive and enthusiasm was due to the string of rejections he'd received the previous day. He planned a morning off to reconnect with why he had been attracted to a sales career in the first place. He concluded that he loved sales and that he wanted to persist. He would work past the no's. The following day, a good portion of his drive to succeed was back. Smiling, he picked up the phone to begin making calls.

You will note in these actual examples that these individuals identified the hurdles facing them, planned their approach around them, and then executed. In other words, after taking stock of their situation or circumstance, they moved forward in a conscious, willful, and deliberate fashion.

It's helpful to recognize that occasionally, the best action you can take may be to do nothing for the time being. The key to differentiating between when to move and when to just observe is to briefly study the situation you are in and determine how things might improve on their own or how the block might resolve itself.

Here's an example to illustrate:

> Cindy realized she was avoiding asking her sales manager about the senior account manager job and if he thought she was ready to be promoted. Cindy was afraid he might tell her no and that she would be disappointed. She had been turned down once before. She decided the best course of action would be to wait for a week and see if her company offered her the job. If it didn't, she would tell her boss she was interested in

the opportunity during their one-on-one forecasting meeting. Cindy felt waiting for a few days would allow her to be more objective about the new position and would allow her time to plan for a successful career conversation with her manager.

Generally speaking, when you can identify two advantages for waiting, it's likely a sound strategy. At the same time, examine your reasons for sitting still and how excuses might be holding you hostage.

To a great extent, we all contribute to, maintain, and influence our present set of circumstances. Are we advancing or sliding backward? Either way, the time will go by. At some future date, we can be ahead of the block or still behind it. What you do makes all the difference.

The world, and our galaxy, is in trajectory. From the smallest subatomic quark particle to Jupiter, the largest planet in our solar system, there is constant vibratory activity. Nature always has a plan to evolve. Forward motion puts you in sync with the greatest movement of the universe. When you take right action, you are working with unstoppable sales power.

21

Seller Beware

Today's buyer largely controls the sales process. If you are a real estate agent, prospective clients have likely researched the local housing market, your firm, and your reputation. In the case of a hot dog vendor, customers may have commented online in real time about the quality, tastiness, and price of their lunches. Purchasers arrive at your physical or virtual storefront with clear ideas about what they want and specific questions about the product.

A few years ago, a woman buying a new bicycle would visit a shop she identified in the Yellow Pages. Focused on moving product, the eager salesperson endeavored to have her leave the store with one of the floor models. Now, the consumer starts her web research by reading reviews on the bicycle she is interested in, and the store's service reputation. When this individual meets the sales consultant, she has a list of pertinent queries. To the extent the cycle representative understands his or her evolving educational and informational role, a sale will unfold.

The turning tide, moving from "selling" to "helping" the customer, has tremendous implications for how you do business and for your future success. People no longer want to be solicited, pitched, or pressured. Instead, they expect to be understood, assisted, and supported.

If you are figuratively cold-calling clients or mass marketing to them, you are battling a sweeping trend that will diminish your commissions and eventually put you out of business.

Consider instead how you can easily adapt to the realities of today's knowledgeable buyers. The key is to understand where they are coming from and what information they need in order to move ahead with a sale.

Most prospective purchasers have done online research before they visit your establishment or meet with you. Subsequently, they have formed a favorable impression. They are in front of you to determine if there is a fit between what they want and what you have to offer.

Your focus should be on two areas:

- Giving the person the information that will help him or her move ahead.
- Raising his or her enthusiasm for the purchase.

For example, prospect Sandra mentions: *"The website shows this bike available in rainforest green. Do you have a fifty-two-centimeter frame in this color?"*

Salesman Clive smiles and affirms: *"Yes, the fifty-two-centimeter is available in a lovely metallic green. I can have it here in the store in two days. You can pick it up on Thursday."*

Sandra adds: *"I want good brakes for touring with a medium load."*

Clive replies: *"Did you see the 'new for this year' disk brakes in the e-brochure? They feel fantastic; very firm, smooth, and progressive."*

Seller Beware

"Good," says Sandra.

Clive continues by saying that the fifty-two-centimeter frame should be the perfect size for Sandra. He also comments that he has seen the green at the manufacturer's bike show and that it's a gorgeous color, very organic. He has noticed his customer nodding with approval. Clive tells Sandra that the painting process is water-based and kind to the environment. Plus, mica, a natural mineral substance, creates the finishes sparkle.

"Would you like to take this black fifty-two for a trial ride to check the fit? Let me raise the seat for you."

When Sandra returns from the test ride, she confirms the sale. *"I'll take it. Please place the order."* Clive thanks her. He also asks about her touring interests and shows her those accessories tailored to her style of riding. To her purchase Sandra adds a Brooks saddle, panniers, and a wheel generator–powered lighting set. Sandra is excited about her new bike and is eagerly looking forward to its arrival.

Clive arranged to be at the store when Sandra picked up her bike a few days later. He introduced Sandra to the shop wrench, who adjusted the seat and bars to her liking. The mechanic confirmed he had thoroughly inspected and pre-serviced Sandra's bike. The sale included two complimentary tune-ups with no expiration date.

Sandra also bought a repair book that Clive showed her. He inquired if she had her previous bike serviced or whether she preferred to do the work herself.

Sandra was delighted with her purchase. She appreciated the care and attention she received. Sandra recommended the shop to several friends, and she made a point of adding to the store's favorable online reviews.

Scenarios like these are being repeated all over the country. Those leading the charge are keenly aware of the new and exciting sales landscape. Buyers arrive with both knowledge about the product and with their own opinions. Top salespeople respond to comments and questions in such a way as to elevate the prospect's interests. You, too, can do this by sticking with the facts and building on the client's emotions. Slowly, and with deliberate attention, read through the above sales example again, noting what Clive said and did to most assuredly earn Sandra's business.

Cold-calling doesn't work because you are disturbing someone who didn't invite you into his or her world. Canned pitches extinguish the natural enthusiasm customers bring to modern-day life and to your product. Aggressive sales tactics turn away clients who thought you understood how they prefer to be treated.

The more you push and force, the greater the resistance you create.

Seller, beware of getting caught up in automatic pilot by relying on outmoded habits and routines from yesterday. Things have changed. Buyers have established their own comparative benchmarks. In this new space, take a fresh look at how you can better understand, assist, and support your customers.

22

Check Your Altitude

Are you flying high on course or about to crash into the ground? You have both a built in altimeter and a remarkable control panel to keep you on your intended path. In sales as well as in life, you will benefit from checking where you are now with where you desire to be.

Most of us go through our working routine on automatic pilot, paying sparse attention to important internal signals. As a result of ignoring these cues, we may find ourselves in a less-than-optimal position and frame of mind. There is a better place to reside.

Larry, a wealth management adviser, makes sure he is right up there all day long. But not by using drugs or stimulants. Larry takes note of how he is feeling and elevates his mood and disposition at will. You can easily learn to do the same.

HR consultant Lynn has become more aware of the extent to which her thoughts propel her temperament. She knows she can turn in a positive direction by consciously adopting a higher-level perspective. When Lynn figuratively shifts her gaze upward, she sees a clearer and more enjoyable path forward. There is less stress accompanied by a sense that events will unfold for the betterment of herself and her clients.

Consider this type of flight plan for greater success, happiness, and fulfillment. There are three steps:

1. Tune in to how you are feeling.

   A few times during the day, conduct an informal assessment of how you are feeling. The purpose of this endeavor is for you to determine your altitude—that is, the amplitude of your emotional state. Strive to observe your state rather than labeling or judging it. Use where you are now as a foundation for climbing higher. In practical terms, welcome whatever you are experiencing and then decide where you want to go. More of the same is just as fine as rising up. It depends on what you seek to accomplish.

2. Keep the nose of your craft at or above the horizon.

   Utilizing the power of your imagination, visualize being in the cockpit, directing your flight. Leveraging the controls, you can change or maintain the plane's trajectory. In most instances, you will want to guide your craft slightly upward. When you do this, do you sense the lift? Level off whenever you want to. And if you are headed down, you may choose to pull yourself back up. Even very small changes in thinking and action will influence the outcome. When you are totally on course and your day is going well, continue gliding on this current.

3. Celebrate a connection with the universe.

   The space around you continues forever in all directions. And then, at that point, what is beyond the beyond? When we reflect on the concept of infinity, we catch a glimpse of the beauty and wonderment of the universe. Your mind can move outward, too, entertaining limitless possibilities and new scenarios. Safely encapsulated in the pilot seat, quietly contemplate a deeper connection with all that is and will ever be. You are a part of an astonishing world that is forever evolving.

Here are two additional examples to concretely illustrate the approach:

Joan is the sales manager at a large appliance retailer. Between meetings with customers, she takes the time to assess how she is feeling. She knows when her plane is maintaining altitude and when it's heading down. Joan can elevate her mood a degree or two by simply imagining herself in the pilot seat, bringing up the nose of her plane. She just makes small adjustments that enhance her day. As Joan keeps on course, she thinks briefly about why we are here and realizes it's about learning who we truly are. Enlightened, Joan is motivated to give her customers and her sales team top-tier helpful advice.

Stockbroker Troy's sales environment is a chaotic, unrelenting flurry of analytical and client management activities. He loves every minute. In the midst of wild market swings, Troy visualizes being the captain of his spaceship, keeping his upward trajectory. When colleagues panic around him, Troy remains calm and focused. He smiles to himself and pulls back slightly on the control stick. *Being alive is wonderful*, he reflects. By keeping his gaze ever so slightly averted, Troy can better see the way forward. *"I find myself in a moment of stillness in space."*

25 SalesBoosters

Taking everything into consideration, you can get off to a quick start by keeping our plane analogy in mind. For you are both the creator of your own path and the beneficiary of it. Fly solo. Keep your nose up.

Throughout the day, check and sharpen your altitude. You'll notice that your sales world can be more buoyant and brighter than before.

23

Small Gains

While competitors struggled in a flat mortgage market, Trish worked with all her reps to help them boost their product sales by 1 percent per month. Over a three-year period, regional team performance was up 36 percent, an astounding improvement relative to the collective competition's 5 percent annual decline. Manager Trish reflected: *"Great success comes about by meticulous attention on doing small things right. I had each team member do slightly more of what they were already doing well."*

Conservative increases are often overlooked by people who are preoccupied with only hitting a home run. To a certain extent, society has conditioned us to desire and seek out large gains. Thinking big and making dramatic progress is wonderful. Equally so, consistent and measured steps forward will produce satisfying results.

We can learn how things work by observing nature. For the most part, shifts happen gradually. The tide rises, one wave at a time. Trees and plants grow a little each day. A river slowly erodes its banks. Over centuries, the physical appearance of continents change. Have you recently noticed that the universe is always moving and evolving at the right pace?

Highly accomplished sales executives recognize how they can elevate their income by making small but strategic improvements. They have an appreciation for the power of a steady and upward beat, gently pushing ahead.

Beginner sales representatives often place too much emphasis on getting the sale and not enough on the individual actions required to earn the business. After a series of repeated failures, they can prematurely disqualify themselves based on their "lack of success" perceptions. An insightful and skilled manager can help the person by advising him or her to gradually improve each of the small steps that collectively contribute to a yes.

"Discouraging would best describe my first three months selling life insurance," Stuart told us. *"One, two, then three weeks passed without a single sale other than to my sister's husband. I questioned if I was cut out to do this and wondered about my future. My boss's counsel was to systematically strengthen each facet of my presentation and not give up or get down on myself. After six weeks I made a sale, then another. I learned that quiet, steady persistence turns the face of adversity into a smile. Looking back now, I'd say you earn the policy sale by following a client-centered approach, incrementally gaining customers trust and then offering them peace of mind."*

As an experienced clothing adviser, Matthew has been influencing customers for thirty-two years. *"You need to keep reinventing and refreshing yourself,"* he says. *"It's the little thoughtful and goodwill gestures that add up. I write a monthly blog, commenting on fashion trends, what's in our store and what's hot. I buy an* Elle *subscription for everyone on my customer list. During the holiday season I call my clients to wish them a great New Year and mention I am looking forward to seeing them soon. Basically, selling is about relationships. You are either in the process of becoming more relevant to people, or less so."*

From a practical and results-oriented perspective, it's a great idea to harbor a sense of increase in your sales. Envision yourself improving. In your imagination, see yourself making consistent advances. Following the advice of Émile Coué, the famous French psychologist and pharmacist, you might want to mentally affirm: "Each day in every way, I am getting better and better." Even more important than the supporting words is the feeling you bring to the table. Anticipate success. Look forward to it. Then you just need to follow through and earn what becomes rightfully yours. Take one step at a time. Your sales career is a continual stream of opportunities.

If you are to stay connected to life, there will never be a time when you stop moving upward. As long as you can make small gains you will have a bright future.

- Your next door, "under the radar" millionaire struck it rich by investing a portion of each commission check.
- That top condo saleswoman skillfully moved all her deals forward while making each of her clients feel like he or she is her top priority.
- Money-making websites strive to gradually increase site traffic and conversion rates.

Small gains turn into big profits. Are you making yours?

24

Relationships Plus

It seems obvious that sales is fundamentally about relationships. Yet many opportunities are squandered due to communication breakdowns. How many times have you experienced representatives being rude, disinterested, or unhelpful? Conversely, you know the top performers in your field skillfully connect with their customers. Conversations flow easily. They are exciting and productive.

Calvin, a retail sales leader, explains: *"You are either building up credits with people or losing them."* Think about his synopsis statement in the context of your interactions with customers. Remind yourself what you are giving them that fosters additional goodwill. For example, if you are promoting vacation packages, what pictures have you shown that have delighted and enthused the potential buyer? If you are selling musical instruments, what have you told the customer that will bring to the surface more of his or her talents?

Your relationships with customers should have forward momentum, meaning that you are continually gaining more of their trust, confidence, and commitment. The only way you can do this is by influencing their thinking with your words and actions.

The old sales approach had reps telling customers what they wanted to hear. But today's doctrine is more about taking care of people than taking advantage of them. When you provide customers with truly helpful advice, you are investing in the relationship and in the sale. You are securing your exciting future. Routinely ask yourself what information or assistance you are giving clients that they find exceedingly valuable.

Maintain the right balance between advising and selling. This occurs naturally when you help your customer and when you believe in your product. You want and expect the client to enjoy his or her new acquisition. You focus on helping the client select what is best for him or her. As you pick up the buying signals of interest and agreement, you can proceed with the transaction.

Successful sales professionals spend a portion of each day on specific relationship-building activities. They give careful thought and consideration to the type of messages they want to inculcate with clients.

> *"People are so busy today,"* comments Monica, a software solutions consultant. *"I schedule a quick phone call to inquire how the programs are working and what challenges the client is experiencing. I make it a point to mention new updates. All of my bimonthly follow-ups are oriented around making the client's world go smoother and easier."*

> Pharmaceuticals sales rep Bruce advised: *"I stay away from mass marketing e-mails and other unsolicited automated messages. These just annoy customers. With the doctor's permission I'll send along new product sheets, always with personalized comments. When I meet in person every three months with the physician I ask how I can best help them with their practice. Later, I record this information in my customer management database, which helps me stay on top of my core accounts."*

One of our clients perceptively summarized why deals occur: *"People give you opportunities because they feel connected to you."* If you consider for a moment the business you have been given up to this point in your career, it's a reflection of the human bonds you have established. When the sale goes to a competitor, you can be assured that company has bolstered the client relationship more effectively than you have. There may be something that you can learn here and then utilize for your ever-increasing benefit.

Moving up a level, one of the most important relationships you can have is the one with yourself. That is, with the larger universe of which you are an integral part. On a daily basis, you should cultivate and deepen your link with all that is. For example, you could take a moment to feel gratitude for everything you have. You could be kinder to people, including yourself. Or you might observe a moment of silence while you quietly and respectfully give celebration to the wonder of life.

It's great to have arrived here today, alive and well in your vocation. As you progress, be more thoughtful and strategic about developing more powerful client relationships. In turn, you will be awarded much business.

25

Feel Wealthy

In the 1950s motivational speaker and inspirational writer Dr. Joseph Murphy presented a wonderful technique for increasing sales. His instructions for doing so were simple, powerful, and results-oriented. The principles Murphy espoused are as applicable in today's globally connected world as they were in the Space Age 1950s.

To boost prosperity, Dr. Murphy advised the salesperson to follow four steps:

1. Relax the mind by letting go of any preexisting thoughts.

2. Once the mind is clear, focus on the words "wealth" and "success," slowly repeating these two words for thirty seconds. Say: "Wealth, success; wealth, success," and so on.

3. As you say the words, sense what wealth and success feel like for you.

4. Following this short exercise, reorient to your work at hand.

Many of our clients have benefited greatly from Murphy's timeless protocol—after they have gotten past obstacles in the way. While the technique is elementary, simple is not the same as easy. Indeed, if it were, more people would be rich. To provide you with an edge in utilizing this methodology to boost your income, here are the top questions clients have raised about the exercise, along with our explanations.

Question 1: *"While saying the words 'wealth, success,' I start to think that I'm not either wealthy or successful. So in effect, I'm repeating the words without believing them. What can I do?"*

You don't need to believe or pretend that you're wealthy or successful for this exercise to work. All you need is to momentarily entertain the concepts of wealth and success. To clarify, let's use a flower analogy. When you look at a flower, really see it for the first time, you enjoy the experience. You are not imagining yourself as a flower. That would be ridiculous, wouldn't it? No, you are just acknowledging the flower and savoring its presence. You are holding the flower in your consciousness. Do the same with the words "wealth" and "success."

Your objective by completing Murphy's thirty-second exercise is to enter the world of wealth and success and to relish being here. Then you leave and get back to managing your day. That's it!

Question 2: *"I've done similar 'positive affirmations' before. I start out with lots of enthusiasm, but then I start doubting that the technique will be beneficial. So my motivation wanes over time. What can I do?"*

What is being suggested here is different from other improvement endeavors you may have experimented with. Do you agree that it would be nice to have greater wealth and success? Define them as you wish. For some people, wealth represents money. For others, wealth is wisdom and attaining new understanding. Success can be any worthwhile accomplishment or state that is tailored to an individual's wants and desires, ranging from a dream career to achieving peace of mind.

Feel Wealthy

If you concur that wealth, as you want it to be is good for you then it follows that you can be both interested in, and committed to, doing the exercise as it has been described above. On the other hand, if you have doubts about the merits of wealth, you should work these through first. Be absolutely certain that wealth and success are what you want. Once you are there, the exercise provides a medium to experience these feelings. As mentioned, the goal of the endeavor is for you to obtain thirty seconds' worth of wealth and success. That is all you need for now. Whatever else is in store for you will take care of itself.

Question 3: *"I've heard conflicting advice on what a person should be anticipating relative to their ambitions about wealth and success. Some authors advise becoming detached from the outcome. Others suggest harboring concrete expectations of gains and increases. Which is it?"*

Paradoxically perhaps, it's both, but on different levels. From a general, wider perspective, it is a sound idea to always expect the best, yet also to be prepared for obstacles and setbacks. What we have just stated can be operationalized by being optimistic and excited about your future. And for saving for a rainy day, too.

At the same time as you are looking forward to good things coming your way, you can also be relatively unconcerned about, and independent from, the outcome. In practice, you let go of any preconceived expectations when doing the exercise. You focus for thirty seconds on doing the method well. Appreciate that moment.

Note over the next few months the extent to which wealth and success enter your life. Pay attention to other unexpected forms of prosperity that arrive. For example, acquiring new knowledge and wisdom. Or being happy and gaining peace of mind.

Question 4: *"Several of the sales and personal self-help books I have studied suggest that a person shouldn't discuss the techniques or their developmental progress with others. Is this true? If so, why not?"*

Many of the Great Masters have advised the students they have enlightened to follow the utmost discretion with their new knowledge. They caution that the learnings may become compromised or ridiculed if secrets are presented to people before they are ready to receive the information. Therefore, the Masters counsel putting your energy and attention toward helping yourself. Apply the techniques to your life situation. As you do so, the principles will become your truth. At that point you will have a good sense of how best to assist your colleagues and customers.

As you can appreciate, there is a large difference between understanding the presented concepts and invoking them to your ever-increasing benefit. Of course, you have every right to choose to ignore or dismiss the information. Alternatively, you may want to put on hold the teachings of today. When this happens and you return in six months, everything may make more sense and have greater appeal. You will know when the timing is right and correct for you to proceed. In the meantime, keep your head up and stay on course.

Wealth and success: Return regularly and make them yours.